# Table Of Contents

CW00529929

## 08 Hidden Gems

## 18 Parks

# 24 Landmarks

#  44 Observatories

# Museums

## Museum Of Modern Art

Is a must-visit museum in New York City. Located in Midtown Manhattan, MoMA is home to an extensive collection of modern and contemporary art. Admission is free every Friday evening from 5:30 pm to 9 pm, making it the perfect time to explore the museum without breaking the bank.

## The American Museum of Natural History

Is a treasure trove of knowledge and wonder. From dinosaur fossils to exhibits on human evolution, the museum offers a fascinating look into the natural world. While admission is technically not free, the museum operates on a suggested donation basis, allowing visitors to pay what they can afford.

## The Brooklyn Museum

Located in the heart of Brooklyn, is one of the oldest and largest museums in the United States. The museum's collection spans 5,000 years and includes more than 1.5 million works of art from cultures around the world. Admission is free on the first Saturday of every month from 5 pm to 11 pm.

# 9/11 Memorial Museum

The 9/11 Museum is a deeply moving and poignant tribute to the tragic events that unfolded on September 11, 2001. Located in the footprints of the Twin Towers, this museum takes visitors on an emotional journey through interactive exhibits and artifacts that pay tribute to the victims, survivors, and heroes of that fateful day. Walking through the exhibits, you can't help but feel a sense of overwhelming sorrow mixed with admiration for those whose lives were forever changed.

## New York Public Library

The New York Public Library is an absolute gem that exudes knowledge, history, and vibrancy. As you walk past its iconic lion statues and enter the grand Beaux-Arts building, a surreal sense of excitement rushes over you. The shelves are lined with countless literary treasures of every genre imaginable, waiting eagerly to be explored. The vast number of resources available here is simply breathtaking – from ancient manuscripts and rare collections to the latest bestsellers and digital offerings. It's not just books though; this library pulsates with a lively spirit through its engaging exhibitions, fascinating lectures, and diverse community events.

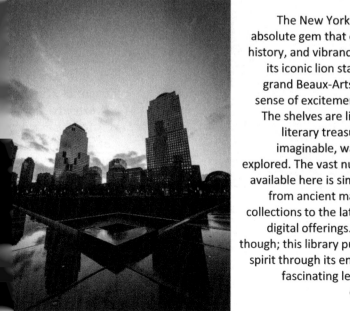

# Museum Of Modern Art

## Why Visit?

The Museum of Modern Art in New York City is an absolute marvel, brimming with a rich and captivating history that has shaped the world of modern art. Since its inception in 1929, MoMA has been at the forefront of artistic innovation, showcasing groundbreaking works by artists such as **Pablo Picasso, Vincent van Gogh, and Jackson Pollock**. It is a treasure trove of artistic brilliance that transports visitors to different realms with its diverse collection of paintings, sculptures, photographs, and installations. Walking through its hallowed halls feels like stepping into a symphony of creativity and imagination. From its iconic architecture to its thoughtfully curated exhibits, MoMA encapsulates the essence of the avant-garde movement in all its glory. Its commitment to championing the most daring and thought-provoking artwork is evident throughout each gallery space

## Top Tip

Consider grabbing an audio tour to learn about the history and importance of all MOMA has to offer!

## Nearby

☐ **Rockefeller Centre**
☐ **Central Park**
☐ **Radio City**
☐ **Trump Tower**
☐ **Times Square**

# The High Line

## Why Visit?

The High Line in New York City is a remarkable urban park built on a historic elevated freight rail line, which spans 1.45 miles along Manhattan's west side. This innovative concept rejuvenated an abandoned infrastructure, transforming it into a lush green space that provides both recreational and cultural experiences for residents and tourists alike. Meticulously designed with distinct areas showcasing diverse plantings, art installations, and architectural features, the High Line seamlessly blends nature with industrial elements. Its elevated position offers breathtaking views of the cityscape while offering respite from the bustling streets below.

 529 W 20th St,
New York 10011

# Bryant Park

## Why Visit?

If you're looking for a chill hangout spot in the heart of Manhattan, Bryant Park should definitely be on your list. This urban oasis offers a unique blend of relaxation and city life that's hard to find elsewhere. Picture this: lush greenery, beautifully manicured gardens, and stunning architecture set against the backdrop of towering skyscrapers – it's truly magical.

It's not just about the aesthetics; there's so much more to do here than just admire the scenery. From strolling around the park, enjoying a picnic with friends, or simply people-watching at one of the charming cafes, there's never a dull moment at Bryant Park. And let's not forget about their various events throughout the year – movie screenings under the stars during summer nights or ice skating on their picturesque rink during winter months – you'll always find something exciting happening here.

 1065 Avenue Of The Americas, 10018

# Hunters Point South Park

**Must Visit**

## Why Visit?

Hunters Point South park is the best place to view the New York Skyline in all its glory. To the left lies downtown, followed by midtown, and to the right, uptown. In one breathtaking view, the magnificent splendour of the urban jungle unfolds before your eyes.

## When To Visit?

Visit at sunset and see The towers stand tall as the sun dips below the horizon, casting a warm orange glow that filters through the gaps. Bring some snacks and stay till the city lights shine brigh

50th Ave & Second St 11101

# Dumbo

📍 **Neighbourhood In Brooklyn**

## Why Visit?

Dumbo, short for Down Under the Manhattan Bridge Overpass, is a vibrant neighbourhood located in Brooklyn, New York with a unique blend of industrial charm and artistic creativity. Its cobblestone streets, converted warehouses, and stunning waterfront views make it a destination worth exploring. Dumbo is home to many attractions such as **Manhattan Bridge View, Brooklyn bridge Park and Brooklyn Heights Promenade**

## Instagramer Paradise

A stroll around Dumbo will give tourists multiple picture taking opportunities, from views of downtown Manhattan to the famous Manhattan and Brooklyn Bridges

# Chinese Scholar Gardens

📍 1000 Richmond Ter, Staten Island, 10301-1114

## Why Visit?

This place is something special! First off, it's an incredibly serene escape from the hustle and bustle of the city. As soon as you step foot in this hidden gem, you'll feel a sense of tranquillity wash over you. The perfectly manicured landscapes, traditional Chinese architecture, and soothing water features create a peaceful ambiance like no other. Plus, exploring the garden allows you to immerse yourself in Chinese culture and history. Each element of the garden has been carefully designed to reflect ancient traditions and philosophical concepts. From the intricately carved stone sculptures to the delicate bonsai trees, every detail tells a story. So, whether you're seeking a moment of zen or simply want to learn more about China's rich heritage, this enchanting garden is an absolute must-visit!

# Parks

# Central Park

## Why Visit?

Central Park is an absolute marvel that never fails to captivate and excite every visitor. Nestled amidst the bustling concrete jungle of New York City, this sprawling oasis feels like a breath of fresh air for the soul. As you step foot into its lush greenery, a sense of joy instantly takes over as you become immersed in the park's vibrant energy. From tranquil meadows to enchanting woodlands, Central Park offers an array of picturesque landscapes that seem straight out of a fairytale.

## Top Tip

If you have the time, spend a full day exploring the park! There are lots of hidden gems in central park so why not see if you can find them all !

## Within Central Park

The park seamlessly blends nature and art, with iconic sculptures and beautifully crafted fountains adorning its pathways. Excitement mounts as you explore the numerous attractions scattered throughout, from the charming Bethesda Terrace to serene boating ponds where laughter echoes through the air. Whether you're cycling along winding paths or enjoying a picnic under the shade of towering trees, Central Park ignites a childlike wonder within you, leaving you exhilarated and eager for more adventures within its enchanting embrace.

# Washington Square Park

## Where And What Is It?

Washington Square Park is a vibrant and diverse public space nestled in the heart of New York City's Greenwich Village. With its iconic central fountain, picturesque pathways, and lush greenery, it offers a welcome retreat from the bustling city streets. The park's strategic location near New York University attracts students and intellectuals seeking respite or inspiration. From chess players engaged in intense matches on dedicated tables to families enjoying picnics on the lawns, Washington Square Park embodies the true spirit of community and inclusivity that defines New York City. It remains an essential landmark that effortlessly blends urban energy with nature's tranquillity.

## History

The park boasts a rich history dating back to the 19th century, serving as a focal point for not only recreational activities but also for political rallies and cultural gatherings. Today, it continues to be a hub for artistic expression with street performers, musicians, and local artists showcasing their talents.

# Times Square

## Why Visit?

Bursting with energy day and night, this iconic destination offers an unforgettable mix of entertainment, shopping, and culture that attracts millions of visitors every year. From larger-than-life billboards to street performers showcasing their talents, Times Square embodies the true essence of New York City's fast-paced atmosphere.

## Nearby

This bustling hub is home to world-renowned Broadway theatres, allowing you to catch a mesmerizing show any night of the week. Additionally, there's an abundance of diverse dining options ranging from casual food carts to upscale restaurants, satisfying all taste buds. Whether you're simply strolling around or taking memorable snapshots in front of its dazzling lights, Times Square guarantees an excitement-filled experience like no other.

## History

Originally known as Longacre Square, it was renamed in 1904 after The New York Times moved its headquarters to the area. Throughout the decades, Times Square evolved into a bustling hub of entertainment and commerce. In the 1920s, it became renowned for its theatres and neon lights, attracting both locals and tourists alike. However, by the 1970s, Times Square had deteriorated into a seedy area plagued by crime and prostitution. Determined to revitalize the district, city officials launched a major redevelopment project in the 1990s that transformed the once rundown square into a safer and more family-friendly destination. Today, Times Square is synonymous with bright billboards, vibrant street performers, and an electrifying atmosphere.

# Empire State Building

## History

This iconic skyscraper has a fascinating history that spans nearly a century. It all started in the 1920s when competing construction companies, Starrett Brothers and Eken, joined forces with financier John J. Raskob to build the tallest building in the world. The construction commenced in 1930 during the Great Depression, and remarkably enough, it was completed in just over a year. Standing at an impressive height of 1,454 feet (including its antenna), this Art Deco masterpiece became a symbol of pride for Americans during those difficult times. Its architectural brilliance and unprecedented machinery like hoisting devices and cantilevering systems pushed the boundaries of engineering marvels. Today, millions flock to its observation decks to take in breathtaking panoramic views of New York City – a testament to its enduring legacy as one of mankind's greatest achievements.

## Why Visit?

This iconic landmark offers breathtaking panoramic views of New York City, making it a must-see for tourists and locals alike. Ascend to the 86th or 102nd floor observation decks and marvel at the stunning cityscape below, including famous landmarks such as Central Park, Times Square, and the Statue of Liberty. The building's art deco architecture and rich history make it a fascinating attraction as well. From its role in numerous Hollywood movies to being a symbol of hope during challenging times, stepping foot on this legendary skyscraper is like immersing yourself in a piece of New York history. Whether capturing awe-inspiring photos or simply enjoying an unforgettable experience with loved ones, a trip to the Empire State Building promises unforgettable moments and memories that will last a lifetime

# Chrysler Building

## Iconic

As one of the city's most iconic landmarks, this towering masterpiece stands as a testament to architectural brilliance and societal progress during the 1930s. From its distinctive stainless steel spire piercing through red brick walls adorned with ornate terracotta details, every inch of this skyscraper exudes elegance and grandeur.

## Inside

Once inside, you'll be transported back in time as you explore meticulously decorated lobbies filled with murals depicting transportation advancements and geometrical patterns reflecting modernity. And don't forget to make your way up to the observation deck on the 61st floor, where breathtaking 360-degree views await.

# Rockefeller Centre

## Art Deco

Its Art Deco architecture and stunning murals make it a feast for the eyes. The centrepiece is undoubtedly the Rockefeller Plaza where the iconic Christmas Tree stands tall every holiday season.

## Something For Everyone

From shopping at high-end boutiques to dining at upscale restaurants like Morrell Wine Bar & Café or Del Frisco's Grille, there is something for everyone at Rockefeller Center. Whether you're ice skating in winter or enjoying a rooftop cocktail in summer, this cultural hub captures the essence and energy of New York City in a truly casual and vibrant way.

## Ice Skate

If you're lucky enough to be in New York for the Christmas holidays, visit the Rockefeller Centre to skate on the iconic ice rink !

# Statue Of Liberty

Must See

## History

This iconic lady has been standing tall in New York Harbor since 1886, but did you know that she wasn't actually born in the USA? Nope, she was a gift from France! The statue was designed by French sculptor Frédéric Auguste Bartholdi and built by Gustave Eiffel (yep, the same guy who built that famous tower in Paris).

## Interesting Facts

Standing at a whopping 305 feet tall and weighing over 200 tons, Lady Liberty sure knows how to make an entrance. But did you know she didn't start off green? Nope, she used to be all shiny copper until her outer surface oxidized and turned into that iconic green patina we all recognize.

# The Meaning Of The Statue

Her crown is adorned with seven spikes representing the Seven Seas and Seven Continents of the world. The crown is not only a symbol of the Seven Seas and Seven Continents, but it also holds a significant meaning. Each spike represents the universal values of freedom, democracy, and human rights that the statue embodies. Standing as a beacon of hope and welcoming immigrants to the United States, Lady Liberty continues to inspire generations with her powerful message of liberty and unity. So, whenever you gaze upon her majestic presence, let her remind you of the enduring ideals that make America a land of opportunity.

# How To See The Statue For FREE

Get on the FREE Staten Island ferry which will give you a great view of lady liberty ! Travel at off peak times for uninterrupted views.

# St. Patrick's Cathedral

## An Architectural Masterpiece

This iconic landmark is a sight to behold, located on Fifth Avenue in Midtown Manhattan. With its Gothic Revival architecture and striking spires, it's hard not to be captivated by its grandeur. Inside, the cathedral is adorned with breathtaking stained-glass windows and intricate marble work. Its massive organ complements the ethereal atmosphere of the place.

## A Place For Everyone

People from all walks of life visit this spiritual and cultural hotspot – whether for a moment of reflection or to admire its artistry. It's also worth mentioning that Saint Patrick's Cathedral has been a backdrop for numerous ceremonies and events over the years, such as funerals for notable figures like Jacqueline Kennedy Onassis and baseball legend Babe Ruth. A true gem amidst the bustling cityscape, Saint Patrick's Cathedral embodies both tranquillity and splendour.

## History

Designed by the renowned architect James Renwick Jr., this masterpiece was inaugurated in 1879. It stands as a symbol of Catholicism and Irish heritage in New York City, known for its stunning Gothic Revival architecture. Despite undergoing renovations throughout the years to ensure its preservation, it remains an awe-inspiring sanctuary that attracts both tourists and locals alike. Whether you're religious or not, a visit to Saint Patrick's Cathedral is a must-do.

# Chelsea Market

## A Place For Food Lovers

Nestled in the hip neighbourhood of Chelsea, this iconic market offers visitors a sensory overload with its eclectic mix of food stalls, specialty shops, and art galleries. As you step inside, mouthwatering aromas waft through the air from various cuisines like sea-to-table seafood at Lobster Place and indulgent pastries from the renowned Fat Witch Bakery. Whether you are looking for farm-fresh produce at The Lobster Place or searching for artisanal spices at Buon Italia, this market has it all!

# Radio City

## The Mecca Of Entertainment

Radio City Music Hall, located in the heart of New York City, is a legendary entertainment venue that has motivated audiences for years. Its iconic marquee and art deco architecture exude a timeless charm that adds to the city's allure. Inside, visitors are greeted by a grand foyer adorned with glittering chandeliers and luxurious furnishings. The main auditorium is nothing short of awe-inspiring, with its breathtaking ceiling mural and signature stage that has seen performances by some of the world's most renowned entertainers.

## Live Performances

From concerts to award shows, Radio City Music Hall continues to be a hot spot for live events. Whether you're catching a Christmas Spectacular featuring the famous Rockettes or attending a concert by your favourite artist, this venue promises an unforgettable experience that perfectly captures the essence of New York's vibrant entertainment scene.

# Madison Square Garden

### The World's Most Famous Arena

Madison Square Garden, also known as "The World's Most Famous Arena," is a legendary venue located in the heart of Manhattan, New York City. With its rich history and iconic status, it has become synonymous with sports and entertainment. Throughout the years, Madison Square Garden has hosted countless unforgettable events from thrilling basketball games and exhilarating boxing matches to star-studded concerts and Broadway shows. The arena boasts state-of-the-art facilities that provide spectators with exceptional views and audio-visual experiences. Its central location makes it easily accessible for fans coming from near and far.

# Brooklyn Bridge

Must See

## History

The Brooklyn Bridge, an iconic symbol of New York City's architectural and engineering brilliance, stands as a testament to the human creative spirit. Completed in 1883, it was the first steel-wire suspension bridge ever constructed, spanning 1,595 feet across the East River and connecting Manhattan and Brooklyn. Designed by John A. Roebling and later completed by his son Washington Roebling after the former's death during construction, this magnificent structure combines breathtaking aesthetics with exceptional functionality.

## Interesting Facts

The two massive granite towers that support this majestic landmark each weigh about 14,000 tons and were built using limestone, cement, and Rosendale cement. Today, it carries more than 130,000 vehicles every day along with pedestrians and cyclists across its six lanes.

# How To Get To The Bridge

The Brooklyn Bridge can be easily reached through various transportation options. The nearest subway stations are the High Street-Brooklyn Bridge station (A/C lines) on the Brooklyn side and the City Hall station (4/5/6 lines) on the Manhattan side. Additionally, several bus routes serve both ends of the bridge. Visitors can enjoy scenic walks or bike rides across the bridge using its dedicated pedestrian and bike paths; however, pedestrians must access them from either Tillary Street or Adams Street entrances.

## What You'll See As You Cross The Bridge

As you stroll across the iconic Brooklyn Bridge, be prepared to feast your eyes on a splendid blend of architectural marvels, vibrant cityscapes, and breathtaking views. On one side, you'll be greeted by the towering skyscrapers that make up Manhattan's renowned skyline. The Empire State Building will proudly stand as a symbol of New York City's grandeur, while the shimmering glass facades of countless other buildings reflect the bustling energy below. On your other side, enjoy a mesmerizing panorama of Brooklyn's charming neighbourhoods and historic landmarks such as Jane's Carousel in Dumbo or the enticing food scene at Fulton Market. As you continue walking, take a moment to admire the intricate details on the bridge itself: its Gothic-style arches, granite towers, and elegant cables far above your head. As you venture across this world-famous landmark, prepare to be enchanted by the juxtaposition of old-world charm and modern urban splendour that characterizes both sides of this truly remarkable passage.

# Flatiron Building

## Why Visit?

The flatiron building is an iconic architectural masterpiece that stands tall and proud. Its unique triangular shape sets it apart from all other buildings, giving it an allure that cannot be matched. Walking by this majestic structure will leave you in awe of its beauty and grandeur. The intricate details of its façade and the way it seamlessly fits into the bustling cityscape are truly mesmerizing.

## The Significance Of The Flatiron Building

Designed by Daniel Burnham, the Flatiron Building's innovative steel frame construction and unconventional shape challenged traditional architectural norms and sparked a new era of skyscraper construction. Its distinctive form, resembling an iron, became not only a triumph of engineering but also a beloved landmark that evokes excitement and wonder among locals and visitors alike. As one gazes at its towering height, piercing blue skies serve as a backdrop for this emblematic structure that beautifully melds history with modernity - offering itself as a visual representation of New York's enduring spirit and limitless possibilities.

# Observatories

# One World Observatory

## Pros

The pros of visiting this architectural masterpiece are aplenty! Firstly, the breathtaking 360-degree panoramic views of New York City from the 100th floor are awe-inspiring; every corner presents a new stunning perspective that will leave you in complete wonder. Additionally, the smooth and efficient elevator ride to the top is an attraction in itself, as it boasts immersive LED screens showcasing the city's history and transformation over time.

## Cons

On the downside, some may argue that tickets can be costly, but when you consider all that you receive, from informative exhibits to mesmerizing views, it truly becomes a worthwhile investment.

# Top Of The Rock

Top Pick

## Pros

Whether it's day or night, the unobstructed vistas of New York City are simply breathtaking. The observation decks offer a unique perspective of iconic landmarks like Central Park, Empire State Building, and Statue of Liberty. Another huge plus is the exceptional architecture and design of Top of The Rock; it seamlessly blends modernity with a classic aesthetic. On top of that, visitors laud the efficient elevator system that swiftly takes you to incredible heights.

## Cons

Popularity can come at a price as crowds may be present during peak hours. But hey, waiting in line just gives you more time to eagerly anticipate reaching this awe-inspiring destination that will leave you feeling on top of the world!

# Summit One Vanderbilt

## Pros

The pros of visiting this architectural masterpiece are aplenty! Firstly, the breathtaking 360-degree panoramic views of New York City from the 100th floor are awe-inspiring; every corner presents a new stunning perspective that will leave you in complete wonder. Additionally, the smooth and efficient elevator ride to the top is an attraction in itself, as it boasts immersive LED screens showcasing the city's history and transformation over time.

## Cons

On the downside, some may argue that tickets can be costly, but when you consider all that you receive, from informative exhibits to mesmerizing views, it truly becomes a worthwhile investment.

# Food On a Budget

## Mom And Pop Eateries

If you want more than just fast food, check out the trendy mom-and-pop eateries serving up hearty portions of comfort food at pocket-friendly prices.

## Asian

If you're in the mood for Asian cuisine, dive into the bustling Chinatown and uncover hidden gems like Momofuku Noodle Bar or Vanessa's Dumplings, where you can indulge in delicious noodles or mouthwatering dumplings.

## Pizza

If you're in the mood for pizza, grab a slice at **Joe's Pizza** or **Artichoke Basille's** where you can enjoy $1 Slices !

## Street Vendors

The vendors are like urban gastronomes, crafting their specialties with sheer expertise and passion. Whether you crave ethnic cuisine or classic American comfort food, the street vendors of New York City never disappoint - they are the culinary heroes adding an extra zest to the city's palpable energy. TOP TIP – For the best prices Visit street vendors in less touristy areas !

# Top Rated Restaurants

## Le Bernardin

Located in Midtown Manhattan. With its sleek and modern ambiance, Le Bernardin offers a remarkable seafood-focused menu crafted by acclaimed chef Eric Ripert. The restaurant's artfully plated dishes, such as the tuna and foie gras or langoustine with truffle and caviar, are masterpieces that tantalize both the taste buds and the visual senses. Le Bernardin's exceptional service, attention to detail, and commitment to sourcing the freshest ingredients have contributed to its consistent recognition as one of the top restaurants in the city.

## Peter Luger Steak House

Situated in the vibrant neighbourhood of Williamsburg, Brooklyn. Established in 1887, this iconic steakhouse has garnered a loyal following for its dry-aged USDA Prime beef that is expertly cooked to perfection. The melt-in-your-mouth steaks, served with the restaurant's signature sauce and accompanied by classic sides like creamed spinach and German fried potatoes, create a dining experience that is both indulgent and unforgettable. With its old-world charm and consistently excellent fare, it is no surprise that Peter Luger is among the city's top-rated establishments.

## Red Rooster

Helmed by renowned chef Marcus Samuelsson, this lively and vibrant restaurant celebrates the rich culinary heritage of the neighbourhood, combining traditional soul food with global influences from Africa, the Caribbean, and beyond. From crispy fried chicken to collard greens, every dish at Red Rooster Harlem showcases the chef's incredible creativity and attention to detail. The restaurant's warm atmosphere, live music, and passion for community engagement further elevate the dining experience, making it a must-visit for New York City locals and tourists alike.

# Per Se

Located in Columbus Circle, is often regarded as one of the finest dining establishments in New York. Under the helm of renowned chef Thomas Keller, the restaurant offers an exquisite experience with its meticulously crafted multi-course tasting menus. The attention to detail, impeccable service, and inventive dishes, often showcasing seasonal and locally sourced ingredients, have elevated Per Se to the pinnacle of the New York dining scene.

# Nobu

For those seeking an unforgettable fusion of Japanese and Peruvian flavours, Nobu, located in the Tribeca neighbourhood, is a must-visit restaurant. Chef Nobu Matsuhisa's innovative dishes, such as black cod miso and toro tartare, have become iconic in the culinary world. The upscale yet vibrant atmosphere, along with top-notch ingredients and impeccable sushi, has solidified Nobu's reputation as one of the finest dining establishments in New York City.

# Top Rated Hotels

## The Peninsula New York

Situated in the heart of Manhattan's prestigious Fifth Avenue, The Peninsula New York epitomizes opulence and grandeur. This historic Beaux-Arts landmark offers lavish rooms and suites adorned with custom furnishings, exquisite marble bathrooms, and cutting-edge technology. An exceptional level of personalized service is extended to guests, with an array of amenities that include a rooftop bar boasting panoramic views, a world-class spa, and Michelin-starred dining options.

## Mandarin Oriental

Perched high above Columbus Circle, the Mandarin Oriental, New York, offers an unbeatable blend of luxury and convenience. Known for its awe-inspiring views of Central Park and its exquisite attention to detail, the hotel boasts lavishly appointed rooms and suites, each providing a sanctuary of comfort and style. The Mandarin Oriental's amenities include a world-class spa, an indoor pool with panoramic views, and a renowned cocktail bar.

## Four Seasons

Situated on the bustling East 57th Street, the Four Seasons Hotel New York presents a blend of contemporary design and unparalleled luxury. The hotel's meticulously designed rooms and suites offer breathtaking views of the cityscape, accompanied by ample space and attentive service. Distinguishing itself as an urban oasis, the Four Seasons offers guests a rejuvenating spa, a lavish pool, and unparalleled dining options.

## Ritz-Carlton

Nestled alongside the picturesque oasis of Central Park, The Ritz-Carlton New York is renowned for its elegance and sophistication. The hotel showcases luxurious accommodations featuring classic decor, marble bathrooms, and spacious rooms adorned with plush furnishings. The Ritz-Carlton's impeccable service is further exemplified through its offerings such as a state-of-the-art fitness centre, a rooftop lounge overlooking the park, and signature dining experiences that showcase the finest culinary talents.

## St. Regis

As an iconic luxury hotel of New York, The St. Regis New York stands as a testament to timeless elegance. Located in Midtown Manhattan, this legendary establishment presents beautifully appointed rooms and suites adorned with custom-made furnishings, crystal chandeliers, and artwork from prominent artists.

# Money Saving Accommodation Tips

## Stay Outside Of The Hotspots

When it comes to finding the cheapest places to stay in New York, there are a few neighbourhoods that come to mind. The first one is **Queens**. Not only does it offer affordable accommodation options, but it also has excellent public transportation connections to Manhattan. Another area worth considering is **Brooklyn**, specifically neighbourhoods like **Williamsburg** or **Bushwick**. These vibrant and trendy areas have seen rapid development recently, making them popular choices for budget-conscious travellers. And lastly, you might want to check out **Harlem** in Manhattan. This historically rich neighbourhood offers affordable lodging options while providing a unique cultural experience that's hard to beat.

## Use Airbnb

From cozy apartments in trendy neighbourhoods like Williamsburg or Greenwich Village to luxurious penthouses with stunning skyline views, there's something for everyone. And let's not forget about the added perks – staying in an Airbnb gives you a chance to experience authentic New York living, as you're often surrounded by local haunts, charming cafes, or hipster bars just a stone's throw away. Staying in an Airbnb will also give you the opportunity to meet likeminded travellers!

## Time Your Visit

Strategic timing is essential when planning a trip to New York. The city experiences peak tourist seasons during the summer and around major holidays, leading to a surge in accommodation prices. To obtain more favourable rates, consider visiting during off-peak months, such as late winter or early spring. Taking advantage of midweek bookings can also help secure discounts, as many hotels offer lower rates during weekdays when demand is lower.

## Stay In A Hostel

Another fantastic option is to book a room in a hostel instead of a pricier hotel; many offer private rooms at reasonable rates.

# Itineraries

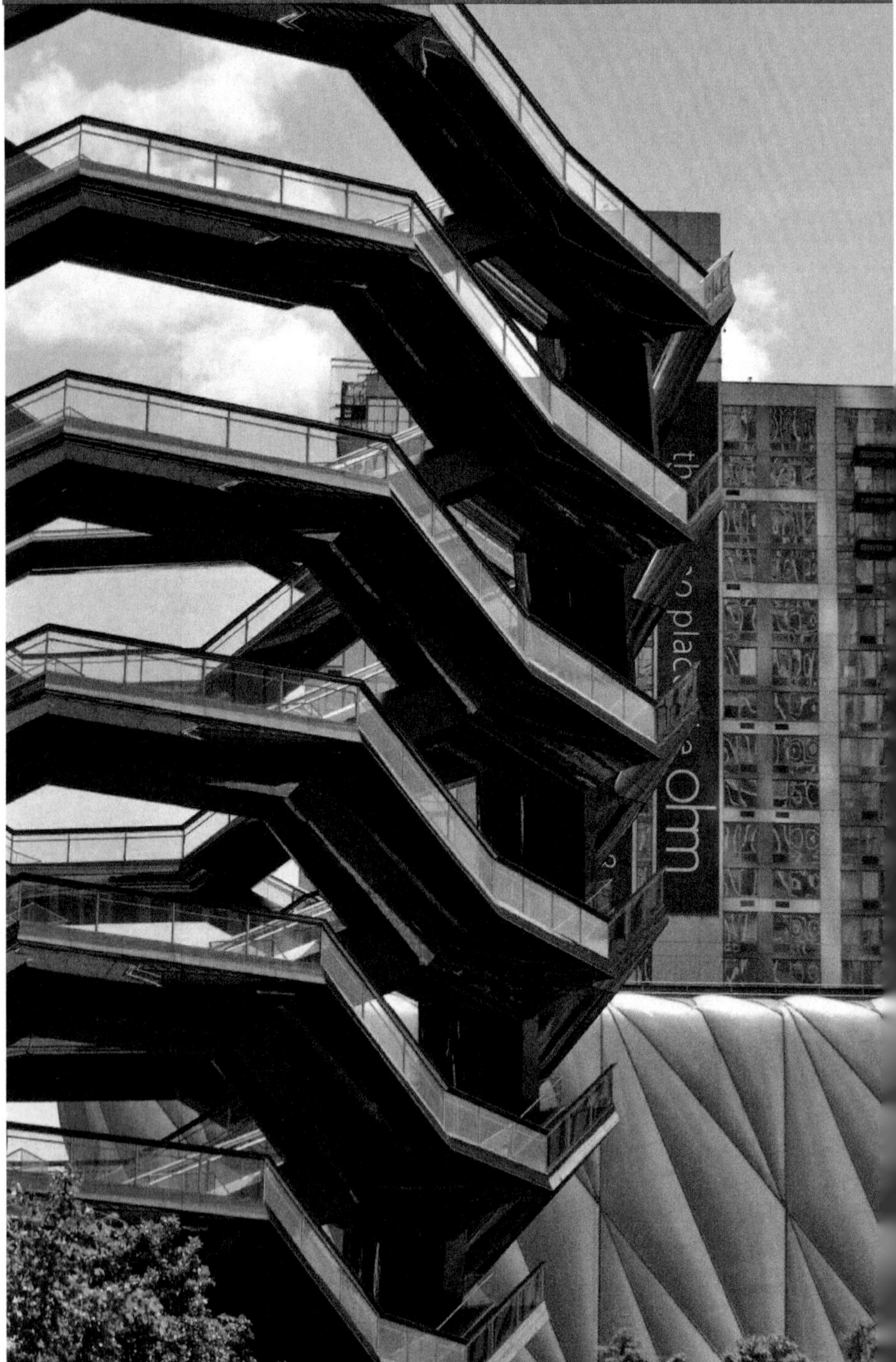

# 3 Day Itinerary

## Day One – Midtown Manhattan

Start with a visit to the iconic **Empire State Building**, where you can ascend to the observation deck for breathtaking, panoramic views of the city.

Next, head towards bustling **Times Square**, known for its dazzling billboards and vibrant energy.

Up next explore the nearby **Museum of Modern Art (MoMA)**, home to an extensive collection of contemporary art masterpieces from renowned artists such as Van Gogh, Warhol, and Picasso.

Afterwards, take the opportunity to catch a **Broadway show**, experiencing the world-class talent that makes the city famous.

Conclude the day by strolling through **Central Park**, an oasis amidst the concrete jungle, offering picturesque landscapes, reservoirs, and famous landmarks like Bethesda Terrace and Strawberry Fields.

# Day Two – Downtown Manhattan

Start with a visit to the poignant **9/11 Memorial and Museum**. This commemorative site honours the victims and provides an insight into the tragic events that unfolded on September 11, 2001.

Next, head towards the historic **Wall Street**, home to the New York Stock Exchange and the iconic Charging Bull statue.

Traverse over the **Brooklyn Bridge** on foot, enjoying breathtaking views of the city skyline and Brooklyn's charming neighbourhoods.

Explore the trendy **DUMBO** area, known for its artistic vibe, independent boutiques, and stunning waterfront views.

Finally, end the day with a visit to the iconic **Statue of Liberty and Ellis Island**, immersing yourself in the history and symbolism of American immigration.

# Day Three – Uptown Manhattan

tart with a visit to the **Metropolitan Museum of Art (the MET).**
his world-renowned museum boasts an extensive collection
panning 5,000 years, from Ancient Egypt and classical civilizations
• more contemporary works.

fterward, explore the Upper East Side's Museum Mile, where you
in discover cultural gems like the **Guggenheim Museum**, housed in
1 architectural masterpiece designed by Frank Lloyd Wright.

ontinue the cultural immersion with a visit to the nearby **Museum
the City of New York**, dedicated to preserving and celebrating
e city's vibrant history.

include your Uptown journey by taking a leisurely stroll through
entral Park's northern section**, relishing in the tranquillity of the
nservatory Garden or visiting the iconic **Harlem** neighbourhood
nowned for its rich African-American cultural contributions.

# 5 Day Itinerary

## Day 1: Downtown's Energetic Spirit

Begin your adventure by immersing yourself in the bustling surroundings of downtown Manhattan. Start with an early visit to the **Statue of Liberty** and the nearby **Ellis Island**. These iconic landmarks embody the spirit of American history and immigration. Afterwards, explore **Battery Park**, enjoying the scenic views of New York Harbor.
Following this, head to the Financial District to witness **Wall Street** and the Charging Bull. A trip to the **National September 11 Memorial and Museum** will offer a profound experience as you delve into the city's resilience. Conclude the day with a trip to the lively neighbourhood of **Chinatown**, where you can savour the diverse culinary delights, this multicultural hub has to offer.

## Day 2: Midtown's Iconic Gems

Begin day two by visiting the cultural hub of Midtown Manhattan. Marvel at the Art Deco architecture of the **Empire State Building** before taking a stroll along the renowned Fifth Avenue. Visit the world-famous **Rockefeller Center**, ascend to the **"Top of the Rock"** observation deck for breathtaking panoramic views of the city, and be captivated by the dazzling art installations at **MoMA (Museum of Modern Art).** In the afternoon, explore the enchanting beauty of **Central Park**. Take a leisurely bike ride or stroll through its vast greenery, making sure to visit **Bethesda Terrace and Strawberry Fields.** End the day at **Times Square**, where the vibrant lights and bustling atmosphere epitomize the excitement of New York City.

# Day 3 — Cultural Extravaganza

Today, discover the cultural treasures of New York by exploring its various museums. Begin with The **Metropolitan Museum of Art (MET),** an unrivalled institution boasting vast collections from across the globe. Spend the afternoon exploring the **Guggenheim Museum**, notable for its avant-garde architectural design and diverse exhibitions.

Later, venture to **Harlem**, a neighbourhood renowned for its rich history and vibrant arts scene. Immerse yourself in the African American heritage by visiting the **Apollo Theatre** and enjoying a soulful gospel music performance in a local church.

# Day 4: Brooklyn's Buzz And Elegance

Indulge in the unique charm of **Brooklyn**, often considered Manhattan's hipster cousin. Start the day with a walk across the majestic **Brooklyn Bridge**, offering stunning views of the city skyline. Explore the trendy neighbourhoods of **DUMBO** and **Williamsburg**, where you can sample gourmet food from artisanal eateries and discover local boutiques.

In the afternoon, visit the **Brooklyn Museum**, the second-largest museum in New York City, housing an extensive collection of art from various cultures and periods. Conclude your day in **Brooklyn** with a relaxing stroll through **Prospect Park**, enjoying the tranquil atmosphere and vast green spaces.

# Day 5: Serene Oases & Cultural Enclaves

On the final day, immerse yourself in the serenity of New York's lesser-known treasures. Begin by visiting the iconic **High Line**, a converted elevated railway turned park, offering stunning cityscape views and innovative art installations. Explore the charming neighbourhood of **Greenwich Village**, renowned for its bohemian ambiance, quaint streets, and **Washington Square Park**. Conclude your journey with a trip to the culturally diverse borough of **Queens**. Visit the **Queens Museum**, home to the famous Panorama of the City of New York, and explore the vibrant ethnic enclave of Flushing, offering authentic Asian cuisine and a unique shopping experience.

# Transportation

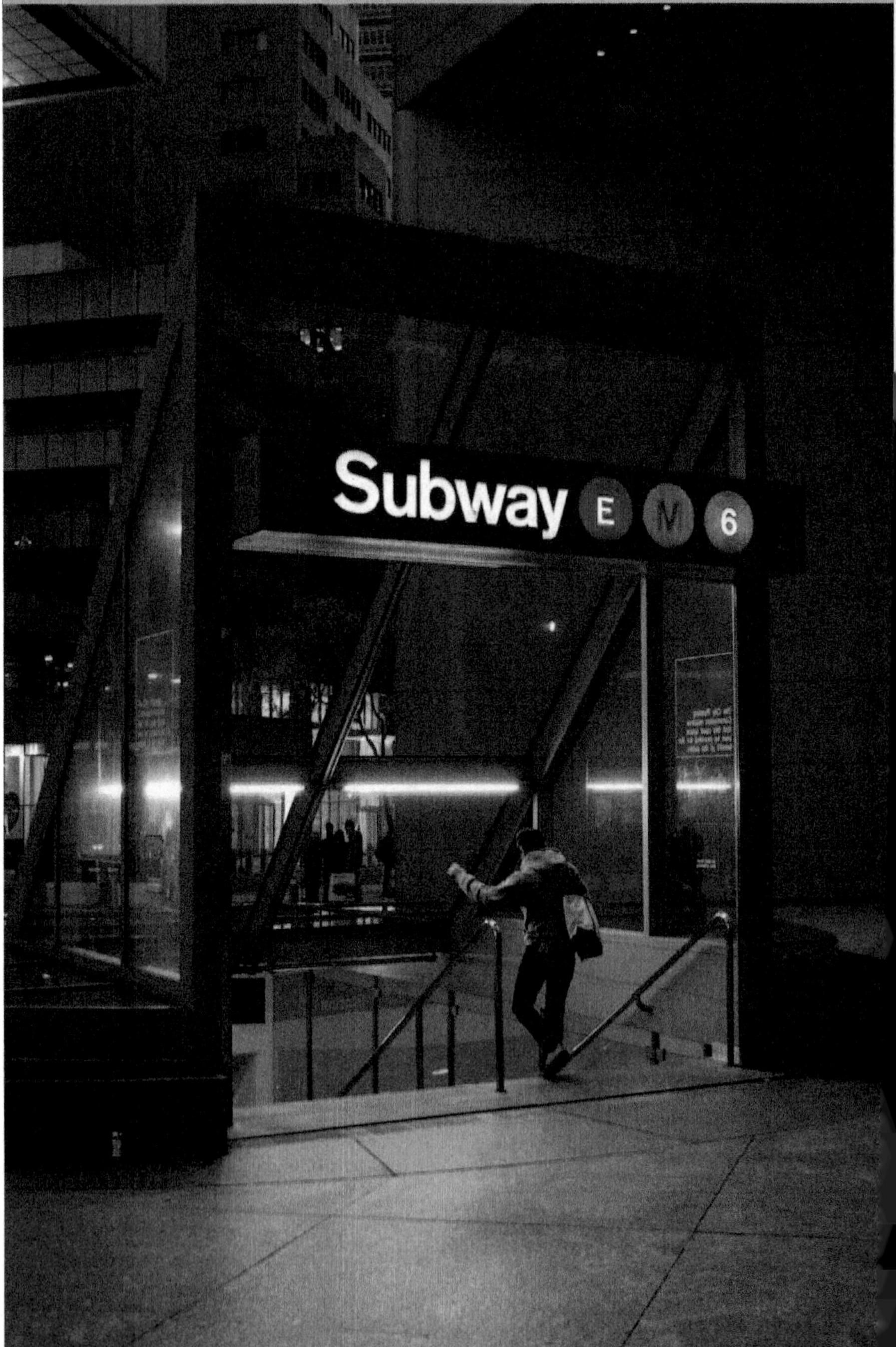

## Convenience

Spanning 472 stations and over 665 miles of track, it is the largest subway system in the United States and one of the most extensive in the world. Serving millions of passengers each day, the subway offers a convenient and affordable way to navigate the city. With its comprehensive network spanning all five boroughs, it seamlessly connects various neighbourhoods, allowing for quick travel across the city.

### Top Tip -

For specific travel routes use a navigation app such as Google or Apple maps !

# Subway system

## Not Just A Form Of Transportation

While the New York subway is an engineering marvel, it also serves as a microcosm of the city's diversity and culture. The subway cars become a melting pot of people from all walks of life, reflecting the vibrant essence of New York. Passengers are able to witness a rich tapestry of cultures, languages, and experiences ! The subway system is not just a means of transportation but a testament to human intelligence, urban planning, and adaptability.

# Buses

## How To Use New York Buses:

Make sure you have a **MetroCard** handy because it's the only way to pay your fare; cash is not accepted on buses anymore.

When waiting at a bus stop, be sure to check the marquee for the route number and destination displayed above the windshield.

Once your bus arrives, hop onboard through any of the doors and swipe your MetroCard at one of the readers.

If you're unsure about your stop, don't hesitate to ask the driver or look out for announcements on audio/visual systems that indicate upcoming stops.

### Top Tip:

During peak hours, buses can get pretty packed, so make sure to move towards the back to create space for others.

And remember, always keep an eye out for your intended stop and pull one of those yellow cord hanging from above when it's time to get off.

# Taxis

## How To Use New York Taxis:

Always check if the taxi's roof light is on or the number on top of the cab is illuminated.
If it is, then it means the taxi is available for hire. When hailing a cab, step to the curb and raise your hand high to ensure visibility.
While many taxis accept credit cards nowadays, it's still best to carry cash for smaller fares or in case of card machine malfunctions.
And remember to tip around 15-20% of the total fare when reaching your destination; tipping is customary in New York City.

## Top Tip:

Try to avoid the use of taxis as they can be expensive. The subway system in New York is a much more affordable way to explore the city !

If you are nervous about using the public transport in New York City, Use a navigation app to easily guide you to wherever you want to go!

# Nightlife Hotpots

## Neon Nights

New York City is famous for its iconic nightlife hotspots, captivating both locals and tourists alike. The beating heart of Manhattan, Times Square, pulsates with neon lights and giant billboards that illuminate the night sky. Drenched in vibrant energy, this emblematic destination offers a plethora of entertainment options, including colossal Broadway theatres showcasing world-class performances.

## Something For Everyone

Furthermore, the enchanting ambiance of Greenwich Village attracts enthusiasts of various genres, with its numerous intimate jazz bars and live music venues. The lure of these eminent destinations lies not only in their historical significance but also in the captivating essence that continues to draw multitudes to experience the timeless charm of New York City's nightlife.

# Top Picks

❖ **Le Bain**

Located at the top of The Standard Hotel. This rooftop bar offers stunning views of the city skyline, a plunge pool to cool off on hot summer nights, and a DJ spinning groovy tunes.

❖ **Employees Only**

For a more intimate experience, head to Employees Only in the West Village, where mixologists craft delicious cocktails behind an unassuming tarot card-reading storefront.

❖ **The Backroom**

Located on the Lower East Side, the backroom is known as one of the last remaining prohibition-era bars with its secretive entrance and retro ambiance.

❖ **Output**

If dancing is your thing visit Output in Brooklyn with its thumping beats and world-class DJs.

❖ **Rusty Knot**

For a classic, understated experience, head to The Rusty Knot in Greenwich Village. This nautical dive bar exudes a relaxed vibe with its rustic decor and waterfront views.

# Artistic Expression

## Evening Art

In addition to its prominent nightlife venues, New York City serves as a melting pot for artistic expression during the night. Art enthusiasts can explore the visual marvels of renowned galleries, such as the Museum of Modern Art or the Guggenheim Museum, which often host captivating exhibitions and events after dusk.

## Pop Up Experiences

The city's thriving underground art scene reveals itself in the form of clandestine galleries, innovative installations, and immersive pop-up experiences. All these manifestations of artistic expression contribute to the vibrancy and creative spirit that envelops the city's nightlife, making it a breeding ground for groundbreaking ideas and unconventional experiences.

# Socialising And Networking

## Opportunities For Connections

Not only does New York City's nightlife offer a platform for entertainment and artistic indulgence, but it also provides a dynamic space for socializing and networking. The city's livewire energy fosters opportunities for connections and encounters that transcend boundaries. Chic rooftop bars, speakeasies, and members-only clubs serve as meticulously curated spaces where professionals from various industries converge.

## Artistic Encounters

For those seeking a more cultural and intellectual experience, art galleries are an ideal spot to network and socialize with like-minded individuals. Chelsea, in particular, is renowned for being New York City's art district, featuring countless contemporary art galleries and exhibitions. Attending gallery openings and art events not only provides an opportunity to appreciate artistic works but also serves as a perfect setting to engage in stimulating conversations and establish connections with fellow art enthusiasts and professionals.

www.GuidedWander.com

**Follow Us @GuidedWander**

## Our mission

With a passion for exploration and sharing authentic travel experiences, we strive to inspire wanderlust in individuals worldwide. Through meticulous research and firsthand experience, we curate tailored itineraries that cater to diverse preferences and budgets.

Accompanied by captivating visuals and engaging narratives, our travel guides offer invaluable tips, recommendations, and hidden gems unknown to the typical tourist. We prioritize sustainable tourism practices by supporting local businesses and minimizing environmental impact wherever possible.

By providing exceptional guides and fostering immersive journeys, we aim to create unforgettable memories that last a lifetime. Join us on this remarkable voyage of discovery as we unlock the world's wonders together.

## " Life Is About Courage And Going Into The Unknown "

Printed in Great Britain
by Amazon

39567191R00046